Also, Woman

Poetry for Humans Born of Woman

CC Miller

Copyright 2023 by CC Miller, LLC

All rights reserved. This book or any portion thereof may not be reproduced or used in any manner whatsoever without the express written permission of the publisher except for the use of brief quotations in a book review.

CC Miller, LLC

Charlotte, NC, USA

CCSaidThat.Com

Print ISBN: 979-8-218-16013-5

Ebook ISBN: 979-8-9884217-1-9

Hello BeLoved. I don't know where you're starting in the trilogy, but this is book three of a collection of a few afterthoughts I like to think of as poetry. Also, Woman was an organic progression from Also, Hi – A Collection of Romance and Revelation and Also, Whole because, spoiler alert, whole time I've been writing the meaningful and universal truths I experience or eye-witness, I am also, woman and my perspective, while obviously not shared by every woman, has a feminine lens. Naturally, I would end up here, with that lens on highest setting. I tried to avoid it. I said that Also, Whole would be my last published work of poetry. (I miss my leisure time with other forms of art.) But, as my dear sister Selinda put it, I am also human, and I changed my mind. As my dad, Raymond put it, I am also, woman so changing my mind is my prerogative. So, here you are and here I am. I hope you are as happy about that as I am.

This project was meant to be a culmination of the insights gained via experience in this chaotic and tenacious world as a member of the feminine sex. Even as I write this, pressing the enormous weight of all that encompasses into brevity and clarity of a few pages feels like a metaphor for the experience of womanhood. At some point, though, I simply had to call it finished. For now.

Table of Contents

Baby girl 2

Daddies and daughters 4

Paper doll 5

Girl gone good 7

Pacifiers and Radio Flyers 8

Possessed 11

Goals 12

Mama 13

Stretchmarks say 15

Searing 17

Surrogate 19

Complaint 21

Wonder Woman 23

Untitled 24

Wrinkle in Time 26

More beautiful 27

I want flowers 28

Where love comes from 30

What we're made of 32

Together 34

Woman's work 35

Dangerously carefully 36

Woe man bashing 39

Flinch 41

A great swell 43

Rose 45

Second and secret streets 46

Experience sis 47

I didn't mean it 48

No competition 50

Sister 52

Auntie life 53

Mine 54

I know (Codependency) 56

She noticed 59

The after wife 61

Lonely	62
Spring calls me	66
Forehead kisses call me princess	68
Suppose (Little song)	70
mute	72
One	74
Legacy	75
Plein Air	76
Heart	77
Earth	78
Earth reclamation	80
River	81
HERmonally	83
Never satisfied	84
I've been sleeping on you	85
I heard a rumor	87
I'm there	89
Polite, not flirting	90
I can't	91
The R-nought of abuse - *An Essay and a Poem*	95
White vanned	97
Smile responsibly	98

Grip	99
I'm proud of you	101
PSA	103
Arguing	104
Easy beauty	107
Weeping body	109
And I don't know	111
I canTeach	113
Pained prettily	115
Pretty	116
When sugar boils	117
Things she wants you to know	118
He didn't ask	121
Future	122
Triggered	123
Hard	124
I'm not her	127
Shame	128
Indestructibly you	129
And Let's Not Forget	131
Know this	132
They'll Write	134

Baby girl

Conceived in poetry
embryonic symbolism
The rhythm of legacy coming
next gen sequencing

Composed of the music of seashells in low tide

Correspondence of all her mothers' mothers and all her daughters' daughters
A truth to tell and be told

She rhymes with life
before signs of life can be detected
Her sonogram an anagram
Earth and heart
extremes and betweens
Her tiny body an echo
The wounded womb of a world protected by a fiery spinning sword

A multiverse breathing, eating, no
Devouring anyone who dares make eye contact
Triumphant
Calamities conquered by her coo

She is power's answer and question

Siphoning willpower with a gaze that drips syrupy of curiosity filling the place your resolve evacuates

Crawling, a prologue
She's going places you want to study

Content with her content
She is the confidence of ages
Beckoning you be far enough away to be close to her Introduction
to once upon a time with adequate awe and caution

She is walking suspense stabilized
Seeding wonder and fear in her wake
Flowering fantasies for her vase

Wandering wild her favorite pastime
Her dominion the minds of the man in mankind
No wonder they seek her domination
God could not have given them a more exquisite kingdom than the nation of she

All is her
She is baby girl

      Pardon me while I geek out a bit. We've learned so much about ourselves and our ancestry through genetics and, still, there's much to know. What we know about baby girls is that they are past, present, and future as they carry the eggs from the first woman into the future and, with every birth of a new infant daughter, new futures are born with a twin hope. Even when the new futures have the audacity to look or act more like dad, they carry mtDNA, made entirely of dna passed only from baby girl who grows into a mother and gives birth to a child. And what does that mtDNA pass down even if not mom's face? Truth. Power. Stability.

Daddies and daughters

From birth to full grown
Daughters, Daddies' quid pro quo
What will be and was

Worry ink blots best
Imposition of meanings
His own Rorschach test

His own extension
His very own projection
Forgiveness, judgment

Incorrigible
Gold wings and iron anchors
Inexorable

Achilles' real heel
Also the crown of victors
Daddies and daughters

    Can I tell you a story, BeLoved? I scoured my early childhood for proof that my daddy had displayed love matching an iota of the adoration I have for him. I can't put my finger on an event or an action. I just know and always knew my daddy loved me. That's precious to me. There's another thing to be said for having those events and actions, though. Observing the dad that didn't have to be care about me in ways no one earthly really taught him to has given me a cherished gift.

Paper doll

Careful, loving, chubby fingers
Not quite grown into dexterous motion
Fool you into believing otherwise
Ambling scissors contour couture

Gardenia in her hair
Shoes perfectly paired
A paper doll, college ruled appears
Colored slightly but boldly outside the lines

If she is perfect
If she is pretty
If she is impressive
She won't be left behind

Left out
Or worse,
Included
Expected

Targeted
A distraction of merciless recreations

Coordinates of care
Clipped in delicate angles
Minding all the features
Inking finer details

Loving all her hunger
Loving all her hurt

Embodying every ember
Righting all the wrong

Coloring, cutting, taping together
A better paper doll

you don't
know what
love is
If you don't
put up a fight

What better weapon for a toddler
Fighting for the love of her life

    During play we learn. But we also teach. How we care for the things we're gifted or the things we craft is a lesson in reflection to our future self. Early on, there was an attempt made to find self-love, to secure a bourgeoning self-respect the best way a three-year old girl could. There's a lot of context missing here, and I apologize for that, BeLoved. Maybe that's a book for another day. What I'd like for you to take away is that you deserve credit for what your little self knew of loving you. Now, your present self can take it from here.

Girl gone good

Good girl gone bad
gon see forever
In the strength of a mercy that can't be measured
What are odds to the true God
What are statistics to a social misfit
She went
From defying Him to defying them
And was resurrected
In a revolution from sin
All for accepting an honest invitation
Bad girl gone good
The pudding's proof
She will what He wills
God willing
Girl gone good
Gon see forever

… *Pacifiers and Radio Flyers*

When I lost the landing strip for my love
I landed on you
You were clear, safe, and I didn't mind the view from where you stood

'Cause one thing about me is I'm really good at loving and you're something like amazing at many things

Over weeks of firsts, I discovered I could do worse than to see if you might be good at loving me

Progressively it became less a question of could, but would, or should

Ideally, I wouldn't idealize but I have a perpetual hope in love that won't die so
My future fantasized a few things I could realize in terms of paradise
My heart spoke so highly of you that my mind could do nothing but stare up at the pedestal
wondering about picket fenced real estate in the sky

But you were just a really nice guy when I could really use a nice guy
Not a landing site but a pacifier
And I was still learning the difference between 767s and Radio Flyers

I was still toying with the idea of loving me and not really taking off
Not really walking in it, much less, catching wind above the clouds
You could've only been as good at loving me as I was, but

Holding the idea of us in my mouth was enough to keep me safe on

the ground
Away from what might've fallen out without you to hold me in while holding me down

I was already leaking so much from being unplugged
Emptied out as soon as anyone poured in
I suppose it wasn't fair to ask so much of you back then

'Cause one thing about me is I'm really good at loving and you're something like amazing at many things

You were clear, safe, and I didn't mind the view from where you stood
And, it turned out, you're pretty good
In fact, you're among the best of men, my friend
Better than a reliable, go-to pacifier
Enabling my desire to pack a fearful wound that I might love again too soon
Too soon for security to catch up with me in the sky

Am I
 skipping a few stages, agelessly paging through to a wonder and a marvel
from babe in need of pacifiers?
too fast?

Good thing growth garners momentum from the generosity of the giver

I have so much gratitude for you
Providing me with proof that I can self-soothe
I needed you and now that I don't
I love you more

Don't argue with me I do
And I wish the best for you
And the headwind ahead of me might only deliver the amen in the tailwind
but know in the take-off there is a prayer for you likely

'Cause one thing about me is I'm really good at loving and you're something like amazing at many things

    I remember pretending to fly being pulled in a red Radio Flyer wagon. I remember my first flight on a 767. They were nothing alike. It's the way with maturity. You get there and understand that you have never been here.
    Do you believe timing is everything in love? I'm a lover of literature modern and classic. The pros of which are an ardent desire to exceed my reality, a vision that is always more mature than my means, a progression that is rarely still. The cons of which are the impatient fumbling of figuring out uncharted paths, misadventures of being too big for my breeches, and the constant reminder that I can't make others come with me into the reality I'm making. Still, when their reality forces me to terms with it, I can't be mad at who and what they are. I simply adjust who they are to me. No one needs to change, to blame, or be pained in this realization. Their true colors are as beautiful as ever and so are mine. What is there not to love about that?

Possessed

She is a pronoun of the most profound pronounced nuance
Fulfilling execution
A complement and helper
But doer?
Not her
Not anymore
Do her tears as much justice as her teeth
Lest her smile grits or bites
When she says I, don't interrupt her sentence
Ancestress of antecedents and descendant
She deserves to be over possessive of the noun that is her

Goals

How do you spell goals
You spell goals by spelling girls
Removing the O for obstacles so the eye can see
Replace the article with a phonetic form of to be
No, but seriously
She was raised to rise not settle in the sea
It does something to my heart to see
Girls and women presented with a problem
I can see the solution seeded
Budding into a flowering tree
As if the problem is a solution
That's simply been waiting to be handed to them
And you know if she is a woman of faith
Your faith could not be better placed than a goal in the hands of a girl
She will move heaven
And there is no common grave that can keep her from reachin'
Goals

Mama

Mama
Your smile lost weight
But I can tell it's heavy
You hold it up in prayer
That nothin' else falls on it
To be carried

Mama
Don't fold under the ache
Your smile for them
Let them know you still own it
Dole it out at your discretion

Mama
To everyone who thought they stole it
Flash just a lil bit of it
Teach them to extol it in song
Carry the tune of the music in it
A note held for too long
Let it roam hot to cold over the rolling poles of the souls magnetized by its aurora

Mama
That smile is good money
Charge interest for their interest in it
Throw back your head and laugh
As if you're weightless
Witnessing it give more than it takes
Appreciating your grace
Broken bones don't show on your face

When everything is not okay
Just know, for you, I hold space
If ever for a while you wanna
Put down that heavy smile
Mama

Stretchmarks say

Stretchmarks say
Come of age
Come summer
ripen something fierce

Stretchmarks sing anthems

Stretchmarks say
Spandex required
Underwire needed
Say bind against time
'Gainst gravity
Defeat it

Stretchmarks say
Defied it
Tried it
Pried it from its pretentious prettiness
Maybe mangled it but handled it
Say don't cry wolf
Defang it

Stretchmarks say grown woman things
Say birth a nation of new generations and let yo' sundress swing
Stretchmarks say conqueror
Say life tried to rip me apart but I stand still her

Stretchmarks say I made it through battles fought subconsciously
and in my sleep
So I be doggone if I don't make it through the ones I aim to beat

Stretchmarks say I'm branded
Brand new
Brand me
So understand me
I stretched into everything that tried to break me
That's what they say
That's what they mean

Searing

By invitation
incision made
Parting ground
a seed lain
Parched in drought
Refreshed in rain
Without permission
ripped away

Icy searing, soulless pain
Miscarrying momentum toward certain dreams

I don't care about the entry denied to social rungs
Clubs of women who believe vacancy of my womb means sub-par society
That it somehow disqualifies me
That a disease of flesh or faith has resulted in the perceived personal failing

Stamping my common sense unworthy
Seemingly unaware that there's not enough evidence that giving birth makes you a mommy

I don't care about the burden of pity placed upon my uterus as the assailant goes into disclaimers that they "don't mean to pry, but why…"

I don't care that admitting to knowing no more than they do on the subject leaves them feeling like I'm the one who was rude to broach it

It's not as if I didn't try

It's not as if I didn't cry prayers of love
Cavernous catacomb echoed my carnal craving for the sanctity of conception
Or that my masculine counterparts suffer ignorance or embarrassment during these ridiculous hearings masked as conversations

I do care about the icy heat that I remember
Like a memory I mostly forgot but remember just enough to keep it foggy and dreadful
I maybe cared too much to be careful
I maybe dared too much to bring her here so soon
A miscarriage of momentum of a certain dream
Soulless
Searing

Surrogate

What's in a womb
The extraneous pressure of those without

Fetal Future entirely dependent on what she eats
Consumption of the elements forming Forever ahead of us

The inheritance of a hopeful past planted
The genealogist's almanac
Rendering seasons fruitful
Bearing dynasties and majesties

Expectation
Relation
Demonstration of evident realities though not beheld
In other words, faith that can be held

Felt

Object lessons
Sacrifice
Intuition
Innovation
Procreation

Someone's ungrateful son's recreation
A good man's oasis, solace, and release

Surrogate to every beneficiary's legacy
An abstract immortality breeding
bleeding the blueprint of lust, love, and liberty

Amicable and enviable confessions impressing the emphasis of eons of stories
A lexicon of vows, oaths
Infant promises inarticulate yet eloquent
In life and in death

In a womb forgiveness indemnifies the ravages of every life it abandons to choose another
Kid gloves and a lion's share in there

A vulgar, hateful quarrel with sanity and tragedy
As many pardons for offense as can be borne in the shrieking plaudits exiting as Tomorrow

From the womb

Surrogate to every honest excuse and confused truth
Surrogate to every very stoic dramatization
Surrogate to age old youth
The newness restless and eager
Demanding attention

Gravity of oceans reciprocating forces

Beg, borrowing, bartering, and stealing the right to breathe
It all begins
In the womb

    The ecosystem of the womb is delicate and powerful. The atomic bomb metaphor I use for womanhood really is centered in this 8 cm by 5 cm organ. The science of it all is breathtaking. I'll probably include a line-by-line explanation in the audiobook.

Complaint

I can't complain
Womanhood is not a complaint
It's a cautionary tale, a fable, a fairytale and a few short years away from everything it ain't

Yes
I know my role like I know the toll
To pay to play my part and say what's on my mind out of my heart with my chest

Yes
I invest in my business, community sees my two cent, and rest assured my family and my God get the best of me off top, so I take the rest for me
That's my definition of success

Yes
I was raised on the rhetoric, teethed on the negatives weaned off the bottle of belief systems that clipped my wings so this caged bird did more than sing
I lock picked and jailbroke my conscience

Yes
It's hurtful to do a thankless job but I serve a joyful, rewarding God it's painful to unplug from the matrix of men to relax soft and feminine
Aware the advantage might slip out of my hands but the woman I want to be is worth the risk

Yes

It's a cautionary tale, a fable, a fairytale and a few short years away from everything it ain't
I can't complain
Womanhood is not a complaint

Wonder Woman

Even Wonder Woman is Diana sometime
Lieutenant or major, still an Amazon
You are power in your delicate vibe
You are super in your civilian attire
You cuff and lasso love and truth
You are either, or, and both

You can turn a cape into a tablecloth
Set the table and the trends
You have it in you to turn love from a moment to a movement
But don't feel forced to prove it
You can bend time like light so, do it
Paced by prayer you'll arrive when you're ready to get there
Just remember

Even Wonder Woman is Diana sometime
Don't let them force Themyscira's throne down your throat
If ruling isn't your chosen role
But don't forget that it is your home
You rule and you roam wonder, Woman
But even Wonder Woman is Diana sometime

Untitled

Time without titles is all she asks
Time to be no more no less than herself
To identify with something other than tasks
She asks for time to be woman and nothing else

Running gentle fingers lovingly over every hat she's worn
Touching the memories that they've borne
Fondling the future in her fore finger and thumb
She asks for time to give herself a pinch of her love

Time apart from mother to play childlike in parks
Time apart from daughter to mother her youngest parts
Time apart from wife to espouse the corners of her life
Time apart from sister to rekindle friendship between her heart and mind

She asks for time to remember the sensation of her flesh
To rest free of anxious guilt over a patient minute
She asks for time to eat slowly
To trace a wine back to its vine
To swallow delight she doesn't feel compelled to share
To inhale her fragrance free of fillers
To remind her that she's still there
She asks for time to revel in the differences between suds and bubbles
To listen to the music of the name she calls herself
To answer to her own rhythm barefoot, eyes closed
Time to figure out where she's laid the things only she owns

She asks for time to be woman and nothing else

To identify with something other than tasks
Time to be no more no less than herself
Time untitled is all she asks

Wrinkle in Time

Time folds over ironing pleats in eras gone
Home to errors, yes, and imperfection
Also, desire, denial, depression, demarcations of life in laugh lines
Crow's feet tell tales of crying and comedy
Recall the contractions conversations contrived
Pleating pleading to be recognized as real pretty
There's so much beauty in the hills that roll in valleys and dimples
warmed by all that's been weathered
Time lets go of its dutiful ambition
Relaxing into a final object lesson
Sands and dust
Dust and sand
All pulled to the bottom of the hour glass
Folding minutes in gritty creases
Story-telling pleats

    My laugh lines and crow's feet make me smile because I remember how often laughter insisted on creating them and how revolution is as much in something as minor as a parenthesis or asterisk existing where there have been so many tears. Like a lovely afterthought or footnote to the happiness that rested there long enough to leave an impression.

More beautiful

I've never felt more beautiful
than covered in the aromatic secretion of my secrets
Looking into a face clearly pleased with the perfume
emitting a glow of satisfied knowing

A cynical sort of sunshine
settles soft on the eyes
if I didn't know better
I would wonder what they see in me

So beautiful is a knowing love
That wraps wings prematurely freed
bandages and sets the fragility
Deeding the deliverance of full strength

I've never felt more beautiful
Than covered in the knowing love
of the face staring back
in glass

    I hope you're beautiful to you, BeLoved. I do. I hope you know yourself so well that you're not nose deaf to your own smell and that you love who you see in every reflective surface.

I want flowers

I want flowers I don't have to ask for
I want flowers I don't have to die for
I want flowers from the garden in the yard,
from large chain florists,
and the supermarket grocery stores
I want flowers, cards, jewelry, chocolates, stuffed animals and more

I want a card that says how you feel
I want a card with your words in the margin
I want a card signed by you
That tells me what your heart wants to
I want flowers, cards, jewelry, chocolates, stuffed animals and more

I want jewelry that symbolizes regard
For the roles that I fill
For the depth of your love
I want jewelry that symbolizes regard
I want flowers, cards, jewelry, chocolates, stuffed animals and more

I want chocolates because I'm not allergic
And any and everybody who isn't
Wants at least a little bit of chocolate
I want stuffed animals and more
Because you adore
All of my parts and all of me whole
I want flowers, cards, jewelry, chocolates, stuffed animals and more

I don't want you to read my mind
It's a hyperbolic tantrum to suggest otherwise
You don't need magic, but you may consult the Divine
You simply need to be able to tell the time

How long has it been since you spoke love to me
When was the last time you said it in treats
How many times have I said it since then
In expressions exceeding the words and their meaning
How long do you want me to hold onto that feeling

Because every gesture has so much meaning
I want flowers, cards, jewelry, chocolates, stuffed animals, and more
Every thought counted in effort
I like my intangibles to come with tangible tells
That is the standard
And I meet it for myself

Where love comes from

I know your people, your history
You come from
where love comes from
Back 'round the unassuming manicured landscapes of truth
as pure as a camera lens
No director's cut
Just gut reaction to what's in as if it's what's on

I wrote a poem for you once
I wish I hadn't burned it in effigy
Embarrassed at its deformity
I'm not generally superficial but I can do a superficial thing
I wrote that you're my favorite color
And I never used yellow
I think there are colors we can only see in the light
where love comes from

Remember how I would hesitate around you
I wrote about the fool's errand of trying to hear your heart beating over my own
Your noise a peace I could smell like fresh fields
It made no sense to feel like this
Like home followed your scent
But wouldn't that make perfect sense
where love comes from

      People who love out of principle people who love out of lust for power, control, or pleasure tend to find themselves lost. If you are attracted to people who lust for power, control, or pleasure, as time progresses, you will find that their feelings for you had little to nothing to do with you. This might cost you love for yourself if you absorb the loss as your own.

Principled lovers aren't always immediately noticeable. Their love's not always shiny or loud or otherwise tangible. We know they are irreplaceable and maybe, out of some extreme risk aversion, we make them lifelong friends for this very reason. If it would hurt more than we can bear to lose their friendship, it stands to reason, that is the love to build upon.

What we're made of

I know exactly what we're made of
I watched everything we're not fall apart
After going into this thing called us
So amorous

I watched magnificently lit ideals crumble off first
I watched bright dreams disguised as dawn turn to dusk
I dusted off wishes to find that dust is all that was
I know exactly what we're made of

In a panic I tried my bestest to papier-mâché and bandage
It hurt like an internal bleed to manage life as us going different than we planned it
Scotch tape sentiments

Masking tape masks
Duct tape deliverance from this destiny
All failed miserably
Desperately clinging to what we wanted to believe we could be

In a manic fit we both smashed, bashed
Screamed and kicked at the disfigurement
Then fell comatose exhausted
We awoke fingers clasped in ashes
Our us intact but shapeless
We worked at all the damaged bits of trust
Detangled the anxious anchors
Tilted to get better angles

Like a good house

Dilapidated renovated
Sound in structure
Gutted and rebuilt
All its interiors reupholstered

Found we bonded well with soldering
It stank and the heat was almost unbearable
Soldiering on holding nothing but intangibles
But what was left was the bones of forever love
That's how I know what we're made of

Together

When you tear down Forever
You are torn down together
You are partnered through time
Grime sloshed about wildly
 will end up in both your mouths
Out of both your ears
Through seasons and years
When you tear down Forever
You are torn down together

Woman's work

Start with worth
End with worth
That is the job
Whatever the work

Roles, rooms, nor tools
Mass or matter
Ceilings, floors, doors, nor ladders

None of these constructs are exclusively yours
Yield to the yoke that lightens
Even as it multiplies its fold
Celebrated

Woman's work
Never stops
Woman's worth
Can't be bought

Start with worth
End with worth
That is the job
Whatever the work

Dangerously carefully

He said, "do the dangerous thing carefully"
I said, "tell me when that has been a choice for me

I'm a woman and beautifully black at that
I'm never not standing up to attacks
On my shape, my complexion, my mouth, motives, and intentions
My femininity, my sensuality, my spiritual condition

It's so pervasive that I have to stand up to the cutting criticisms of other women even
Myself included
The exclusion for faultfinding honestly sometimes the only inclusion
I'm finding open to me

Just to sit comfortably soft
Is a danger
A revolt
And as a result
I'm a rebel to even consider taking time off

Self-care ain't trending for nothing
It's intriguing
To see a person living outside the walls, doors and barbed-wire fences
Of contentious opinion on just living and breathing

And when it comes to women
Oh, you see her
Raking and tilling her posts with edits for the critics
(I've never seen a man defend his life experience like this)

But sis
Oh, she's gotta explain all the multitudinous ways
she's handling every facet of her business
(And maybe some that isn't)

And why she does or doesn't deserve this
To those whose time seems otherwise occupied until it's time to chime in on her decisions
Where've you been?

Soft-life is a carefully navigated wonder
It's as dangerous as moonwalking a tight rope from the moon to the sun
To be woman

Every heel into humble submission comes at the toe of saying no
to somebody who thinks it audacious that our God granted her permission to have our regard
Somebody disregarding her worthiness
Her heel toe through land mines somebody will mistake for dancing
And reduce her artful execution to his or her mindless entertainment
All too much or too little
And never enough
but beleaguered so much

Just because they witnessed her beast mode
So beast of burden must be her role
A tole for the toll taken
Tax her in pretty
And she should be quick to pay it off
She can just shake it off

But don't take too long adapting

'Cause that's perceived to be a lazy and entitled write off of everything else that she brought to the table
Troubled with reduction and self-deprecation
That a brunch and spa day can only do so much to mend
But yeah, she gon crip walk through the obstacle course
Of course
Loyal in all the things
Barely breaking stride to straighten her crown
Queen
Full time even on her sick days
Else somebody gon have something to say

Somebody gon weigh in on what weight she should and could, if only she would, carry
Bury her shoulders in burden

He said, "do the dangerous thing carefully"
I said, "tell me when that has been a choice for me

Woe man bashing

I said nothing,
I was "hiding something, probably the truth"
I was "fine, just always in a funky mood"
I spoke,
I was "lying and no one could really know the truth"
'cause a girl who's known for making a weapon of truth must "be fast and lying and here's the proof"
I lived it while it was killing me
It killed me in my life's beginning

Remember that time when you were a woman?

When I was told to protect myself from people who weren't going to defend me from themselves
To block accusations of deviancy with legs too short to cross anywhere but my bobby socked ankles
Lest I be labeled "fast"
It wasn't "bashing"

Bows, beads, and braids are "abusive"
Free-flowing tresses is "sexualizing"
Accounting for perverts is against child labor laws, ain't it
My fabric is "asking for it" even when it isn't
My happiness belongs to whoever's clever enough to steal it from my silent screams

When shame rattled my brain against my skull
Disconnecting me from my own love
No "bashing" was found there
Neither was it "bashing" when my insides became alien to me

Cause and effect notwithstanding
Branding an innocent is a more fluid transaction
Than expecting a villain to become fluent in acting with self-discipline

Still, don't remember that time when you were a woman?

All our villains are victims
So, our victims must be villains

When I penned my life from once upon a time
To tell my tales that have nothing to do with being saved by fairies or princes

It was "crazy nonsense"
It was "inauthentic"
It was "masking"

It was woe man-bashing

  This satirical piece was inspired by the adopted term man-bashing. You won't find me shying away from the ills of the feminine realm. Misandry exists, and it's awful. That's not this poem, though.
The misogynistic tones of being called a man-basher for expressing boundaries and/or grievances at the hands of power or authority is an exhausting layer of impossible dust settled on top of mortal danger. And you are not an expert if you don't remember that time when you were a woman experiencing these traumas no matter what letters trail your name.

Flinch

The first time I flinched at someone's touch
I was so proud of me
To those of you who have only ever known touch to be well meaning
Or that you have dominion and autonomy over your own body
This may be something you have trouble grasping

That flinch represented a promise kept
Amnesty
Love for me
That I would know ownership over my self
Better late than never

I'm not the woman who looks toward the cat call of a car horn
The venomous vulgarity in the vanity of the
man who thinks this flatters me

It's not flattering

I start floundering for something to protect me from further obscenities that might be volleyed at me
My obscurity turned celebrity does nothing for my self esteem
My walk was confident before your attentions produced in me an urge to shrink

If it wasn't for my identity established, created, I might let you make me
But I can't think of a higher disrespect
Than to let you deduct me from me

So I force my gait to cooperate

It's awkward at first but when it calibrates
I am so proud of me for flinching

A great swell

A great swell of pity rises for the absentee you who joined your father
Raised one way and one sided you abandoned you in search of him
Hoping to put him back in his place to define yours
You left you alone because he did
You left you to roam
Like he did
You were home alone since that weekend when

A great swell of pride took him aside for a life outside where, when he died
You found yourself not far behind
Ambitious, capricious, and quick to take offense
Especially when anyone pointed out the resemblance
Pushing back and cancelling healthy friendships
In your defense
With him not in place for you to define yours
You couldn't possibly know that the difference between distance and distant is negligence
I mean to say negligible
You're eligible for more

A great swell of happiness for the way you rein in the rains that reign over your pain
Hydroplaning drift arching a lane you can slide in so that you define your place in the universe
You indomitable thing
You needed him but you need you now as much if not more
You are not a generational curse or daddy issues
Issuing forth some congenital defect of deficiencies

Not an expletive
you are an exclamation and an ellipsis
Emphasis on the infinite space outstretched 360° for you to define
yours

Rose

Is a rose bush not simply a thorn bush
which we forgive for its painful defenses
Praise petals their scent and delicate nature
Color, grace, and gentle strength

We don't condemn the bush for our inability to squeeze it with careless hands
Nor do we shun it

We revere it
Lyrically immortalize it
Manipulate our way past perimeter protection
Bid its buds to represent our deepest affections and grief

Declawed of its only security we place it crippled in expensive crystal coffins
await its death with dread that we must enjoy doing it all again

    In the 5th grade, my English teacher Mrs. Carr said, "I don't want to see you start a sentence with "in my opinion". You're the writer. It's a narrative. We know it's your opinion." I've not yet met a perfect human in person. I also have never met a couple who didn't feel the need to state, as if out of some legal formality, that "he or she is not perfect, but…" Why do we fine print people this way? Do we really need to qualify our love for one another to others? How did we get here and can we go now?

Second and secret streets

On second, the urge for first is an unquenchable thirst
Claiming the prize at the price of being the prize is worse

Secret, the worst of all the names to be called
For all the languishing gets so loud

Demanding a pride so proud
A denial of its nature and existence

Ambivalence to the affectation of affections
Builds whole cities of wicked walls

For the streets to feel like home
Less like less than

It's the appropriation of first and foremost
The sound stolen from forlorn

At the corner of Second and Secret Streets

Experience sis

My experiences don't invalidate yours, Sis
But there is an absolute truth that exists
We can dance around it and complicate this
Or we can discover and acclimate to it

The longer it takes to make our way
The more unfortunate experiences we subject ourselves to
Doing what comes naturally is not a foolproof methodology

It's possible to right and unrighteous
But we don't have to be
We can stand on our fear for safety
Or we can fly on faith and be happy

Morality and morale could be equally high,
Freeing
If we both concede to the truth in these experiences
There is an absolute
And it may not be what either of us experience, Sis

I didn't mean it

I doubted
Pouted
Shouted
Outed all your insecurities
Things you told me in secrecy
Vulnerably

Jealousy took hold of me
The older me surfaced
Bitter, mean

Parched of clean water
Ought to know better
But thirst is the worst in drought

About that

I really didn't know I had it in me to rise to these lows with such splendor
Doors open to shut doors
Amend the covenant of friendship
I didn't mean it

How easily the best of me
Cowered in the shadows
Clandestine yet brazenly
Dressed in green throwing shade like trees
I loved the height of my own canopy
More than what we used to mean

Imagining you dwarfed by my magnificence
Darkened by the crevices
Perhaps a power trip
Unbeknownst to me to be vices

Standing on the standard I set for me
Considering any loss to be what's best for me
Collectively, my past lessons cast impressions that haven't left me

I go first
I go hard
Protect my head
Protect my heart

Except for the part that you live in
For that I've got no explanation

You just have to believe
I didn't mean it

     Betrayal, jealousy, and mean-girl behaviors are universally deemed feminine traits. Hey, there isn't even an equivalent to mean-girl that describes the same trait in males. Regardless, it does happen, and, when it does, it smarts something fierce. "Insight slows anger", as Proverbs 19:11 says. In the search for understanding, I'm able to write what I believe is the inner dialogue of a woman suffering from an internal conflict with a friend that is rooted in some of the human qualities we'd rather not admit to owning.

No competition

The way our dna plays out in society
A tendency towards jealousy only gives credence to the nonsense
I paid no more attention to the size or shape of your lips
Than I would to the size or shape of an orchids
A favorite flower

I don't need you to be mythologically exotic
There's no validation in it
My love for me has no dependencies on explanations of our differences

Nothing is added by dividing
Dismiss the denunciation of every denominator greater than one
The fraction missing itself can't be trusted to make anyone whole
Make anything outside of excuses

I don't need you to excuse your existence
To pardon my own
And we are not in competition

I don't need you to be me to love me
Neither is the converse something I desire for you
I love you in all your splendid anomalies
The human race is one global family
I can't look up at or down on you
From where I'm standing

My admiration of your complexion is not deflection of the admirable state of my own skin
Within my melanin are the same elements of clay
From which you were made

The s or c formed by proteins protruding from your head are not nearly as important to me
As whether your kindness is as abundant as the pride you take in your beauty
I don't need you to explain your beauty in terms of origins of ethnicity

But in terms of quality, I already see it
Measure the length of your selflessness like you perform length checks at the mercy of a flat iron
Measure the depth of your dreams against the height of your confidence more so than the ratio of ancestors from a particular continent

You are significant in your brilliance regardless of your defensiveness
I wish you would brush off the random peevish annoyance of insecurity lurking in our neighbors
I am team you and team me

We are not competing

We suffer defeat if we compete in this hunger game pageantry
We don't need to fight or lock the night
And we still have everything we want in life
I own my love for me and have plenty for you inside
I don't need to mirror or malign you
Murdering character serves no benefit
You're my family
Not my competition

    I wish I could adequately cover the pressures shaping womanhood without including a conversation of the divisive elements. We talked about a few of them in earlier pieces, but this piece specifically is about combating the divisive nature of colorism and racism in our inner thoughts so that it doesn't find a place in our daily lives.

Sister

We've been holding hands at heart
A love that converts malady to melody
You're the one who can quickest rile my temper
And quell my tempest

Your name is the one that surfaces
When I need protecting
When I'm feeling protective
There's no such thing as apart

Forgiveness is a past tense for offenses you ain't e'en committed yet
Even if we don't speak for a minute
We are a finished sentence entirely comprised of facial expressions

We are alibis against lies
We are the private truth even if it makes one of us cry

We are explanations understood and reliable
We are you see us even if you see only one of us
We are amens at the end of one another's prayers
We are I can, but you can't because
that's my sister

    Sisterhood deserves a concentrated concentration in the book of woman. It's hard won and worth every tear. It's a beautiful thing.

Auntie life

Some of y'all didn't have aunties and it shows
You can't fully appreciate the love of a mother till you have mothered someone
But auntie comes right up and into the threshold of that love

Aunties are the sanity a mother loses to an infant in utero
But is on reserve to enter a guilty by reason of insanity plea
in a conspiracy pursuant the best life for a nephew or niece

On demand for the plans for that child's fiscal future
On call for the fantastic fantasies he or she might dream up
On the way, any given day, fully armed, fully funded, and fully equipped for the shenanigans, the payback, the commonsense commencement speech, and the retail therapy

Aunties supplement the elements of a child's development
They can ever so carefully bend without breaking a no
They are the fireworks and confetti to a yes

The best friend before best friends get inducted in
Parent without the gravity of parenting
Aunties are the lily pad love that looks like it lives surface deep but is rooted
Out the mud love
And it only ever grows

If you have an auntie you know
Cause it shows

Mine

I put mine down to help you fashion yours
From stubborn determined rocky soil
Raw and chaffed fingers and palms
Opened in the brightest shades of psalms

I put mine down to help you look for yours
Turned over stones
Peeked in windows
Kicked in doors

Many years passed and you were still in pursuit
And I didn't give up on you
Even as your search was pulling you away
In the long stroke of the figure 8

But I decided it was time
I went back to pick up mine

Covered in dust and still a little young
There mine was
Just like I left it many years ago
Took just a minute to polish and shine
And hold to the light
That which was mine

Here you came walking by
Saw me with it and denounced my pride
Chastised me for its natural light
Told me it would never grow up
Hurled threats at me if I might

Nurture what is mine

In time I came to recognize
That what is mine deserves my time
And I gave yours back
To behold that which is mine

I know (Codependency)

I know, I know
That sister you're dating
She likes you for you
Doesn't criticize you for what you've been through
If anything, she's helping you heal, bro
I know
She might go ghost but who doesn't need time alone
Sometimes she acts somewhat single out here
But it ain't nothing you can't forgive
not so bad now that you're used to it
I know, I know

Sis
Thinking about him feels like it's filling a gaping hole in your soul
You've never felt intensity so real
The two of you can weather apocalyptic storms together
Apart nothing even matters
You can't remember who you were before you met
You dismiss it thinking you must have not been much because you elected to forget
I know, I know

Truly, introduction to this person has you convinced they're a god-send
How else could you explain this compulsive consumption
A pert near viral presence in your brain
All you can remember is their name and the smile that hi jacks your face when you say it
I know
You were never this happy alone
I know

It's #goals
So romantic
Sweet
It's, oh what is it called?
Codependency
Where we cross the line of deep respect to self neglect
And give the kind of love that should only be devoted in worship

Jehovah is a jealous God
Historically he guarantees he wants no parts of that cord
After all that Jehovah has done to raise us what must he feel to see us let somebody raze us to the ground from whence we came
Who died and made them king?

The one who died and was made king would disagree
His fondness for us must be crushed to see us excuse the basic principles of love
Just to date SOMEBODY
I know, I know

Sometimes time acts like gravity and the heart gets heavy
The scale says mean things and your medicine cabinet full of pills and creams feels like an exam you're failing but
Anybody ain't the answer
We literally have forever
It's a small thing to a giant
Lions don't lose sleep over the opinions of sheep
Whatever cliche proverb you need
Please remind yourself that there is only one person you can't live without and he's not of this earth

I don't think he likes it when he tells us who we are and we doubt it because some other particle of dust is discounting us
We must know our worth

I know, I know
That's easier said than done
I can't get on the gram without feeling less than the standards set by humans
But isn't that the problem

We already have divine standard
We don't need another one
We're not adopting negative conditioning anymore
We're not rewarding bad behavior
And we're not sending series of epic texts explaining this
They know, they know

We deserve patience, love, integrity inherently
We deserve to feel safe, appreciated, intelligently
No pageantry is a viable substitute for these truths
Whatever you decide to do
Whomever you decide to date
Just make sure they aren't blind to the value God assigned you before you venture to propose
Don't worry, you won't have to wonder
You'll know, you'll know

    In AA and NA meetings they teach you about the effects addiction can have on the peripheral members of the family. Of course, the inherited effects are obvious. Between the two circumstances, there is no one without potential to develop codependent tendencies into a problem. If you look at the friends and family you're trying to make and they look more like a high you're chasing but can never catch, then this one's for you. Been there. Done that. Wrote a poem about it. Probably sell the tee shirt on CCSaidThat.com.

She noticed

Trust me
She noticed
Her nerves registered the variation of verve
and swerved left to reserve judgment

To avoid condemning the man she loves
 to death by honesty
A collision with truth would undo her
 while undoing him

Trust me
She knows this

With more than eyes she sees his
Vicarious visions bowing head and lowering eyelids
The excuse of being tired has grown tired
The intimacy differential treated inconsequential is substantial
enough to shoot a question mark through her heart

I heard arrowheads leave horrible scars

The staff of regret protruding ensures a wound that never closes

She can't hold him against her without holding it against herself
Or else bleed out in the extraction of answers
She's never seen a hemophiliac hemorrhaging
She just knows that's what would happen
if she pulls on that thread

The thread from her heart to his

The snap will snap her in half
How sure can she be of the half remaining
Sustaining a life worth having
So she bites her tongue and holds it

But trust me,
She noticed

     I wonder if men register emotional infidelity the way women and children do. Based on my experience with it, there can be a long distance between recognition and acknowledgement and then ownership may never come. I don't subscribe to the belief that our biology makes it impossible for us to be more considerate humans to one another. If nothing else, we should give credit where it is due and acknowledge that there is nothing hidden from God and maybe ask him how he feels about it.

The after wife

An avalanche of answers
Questions suspended in ether
Either lose air in the former or be swallowed by the latter
Life after wife

Wandering
wondering which painful truth or majestic lie will snowball into catastrophic consequence

Conviction a condensation
beading on the brow in icy arches
Cathedrals encased in icicles
make for a beautiful catacomb
Caricature of character
mocking in the cold winds of change
Crippling the collected
as closure comes in the powder falling

Answers avalanche burying in a purifying dust
Questions suspended in ether swallow up
Neither having the power to stop

Life after wife

Lonely

You're too insert pretty/smart/good to be single
What's wrong with you that no one wants to be with you
May not be what you said but it was what you meant
BeLoved, isn't it
And then you set on a quest to identify it

I'll let you sit with this

I'm not saying I don't get lonely
I'm saying I don't get lonely enough to put up with alternatives
What they thought is I would stay
Like I had no place to go
What they taught me is that they don't stay
So I move like they'll go

How can I let go of what I know for sure
For something promising to be
When promises don't mean what they used to mean
My heart's last wish pours from porous skin
Asking them all for one of them to show me something different
No love

Only more like
Our differences brought more of the same
The off rhythm two step of love and hate
I could name names but who has time
My dreams fill my calendar
I don't have an opening for years
Making up for the pages red x'd with bloody tears

I'm not indifferent or pessimistic
Only a different brand of optimistic
Just feel my time won't be waste trained
If I lift wishes and build an hourglass figure
That doesn't rely on dusty sand to tell the time

I'm bitter sometime
I'm angry sometime
I'm lonely sometime
And they can't guarantee that with them I won't still be
But anytime and every time I've got more time than money
And I spend both wisely
Like mommy taught me
So I'll give it some time one day

I'm not saying I don't get lonely
I'm saying I don't get lonely enough to put up with alternatives to the life I want for me
I like my odds and ends
My odds with God surpass my chances with them being enough like him to make it worth it
I'm not insatiable but He made me thoroughly capable
Durable
Willing and able
Not of or for the water soluble

Built and laid the table so the only one I wait on when I eat is the Amen
Prayin' there'll be no crumbs left where I eat
Complete
Scripturally I can't outrun a blessing sent for me
And I live in view of eternity
My Father knows best when I'm ready
Really

And not just lonely

I'm not saying I don't get lonely
I'm saying there are worse things to be

Spring calls me

Every now and then I get home sick for tulle and satin lace
Nostalgic pearls that drip harder than crocodile tears on card stock
They page me
Calligraphy that may be written in English but it speaks the language of femininity so fluently
it becomes its own kind of Romance language
Arrangements of baby's breath of breath-taking proportions
Floral chandeliers
Blush
Propping up a proper version of bliss
where a kiss has been missing for years
Spring calls me Lonely in the most seductive way

Waddling towards my pov a buttery brown dough creation flashes gums drooling
and even though it's some random little one on social media
the smell of sweet milk fills my nostrils and lands with a thud in my gut
Gutting me of contentment and satisfaction once a month
except for the season heaviest of births when it is all and every reason
The little toes blow me away
Spring calls me Lonely in the most seductive way

Visions that smell of parchment, cotton, and linen
Cherry blossoms
Fresh cut grass laced in the colors of fresh popped bubbles
Matching the choral laughter
As hours nestle in the cuddles of chapters
Enraptured in the lap of masterful brushstrokes

Stealthily replacing the apple of eyes
with every latitudinal fondle
fighting sun for its right to brand Favorite on warm skin
Brooks giggle nearby at secrets
They needn't keep nor say
Spring calls me Lonely in the most seductive way

Forehead kisses call me princess

I felt the kiss on my forehead call me princess
Without him saying it
It found where I founded my crown
The pucker bowed and vowed to sanctify my submissiveness

It relinquished perfunctory into a piousness
a bliss like this can rarely lay claim to
Aimed to raise me as I leaned beneath and into the cushion of its simplicity
Rendering my heartbeat a low, slow percussion

To lay my cares in this cushion is to lay constellations in their positions
In the velvet waters of space

It's no wonder a tear spilled over in the overflow
an after-glow glistening like a fallen star from this forehead kiss
Listening for a calling card from this forehead kiss

Abdicating the old hold I have on previously plundered places
The point of me rotted in stasis
A liberating reciprocal kiss of breath
As if death compressed my breast and let go, inept
If I breathe in too fast, too deep,
I'm sure I'll inhale the concentrated universe to keep
And maybe we wouldn't survive

These things demand a slow savoring

A misty vapor ring wraps round us nebulous while time stops to

stare at the kingdom we made on cloud nine
where a kiss on my forehead rang out royal pronouncements of life
beyond the planted seal of approval

Beyond things that return to dust
Beyond lists and wordlessness
The forehead kiss calls me Princess

    Who was the first person to kiss you on your forehead? Did you just smile? I wonder if men value the forehead kiss the way and with the weight that many women do. It isn't a salacious act. No vanity involved. It needn't be reciprocated in like value to be appreciated in value.

Suppose (Little song)

My faith needs stretching again I suppose
I dreamt of you again, my little song
You wore different skin, darker than before
The color of well-cultivated soil
Rich. Waves and curls cavorting for my crown
You were taller, broader, a gentleman
A smile like glints of moon caught on black sands
You were an answer to all my asks and
Those I had not thought to ask as of yet
It started as a blissful dream of me
Busy fulfilling Bible prophecy
Not even noticing you notice me
Until the moment you chose to make known
To introduce yourself, my little song

Publicly and undeniably us
Like a winning hand of cards dealt face up
Not a question mark in sight for future
Not made of many, but of the right words
A comfort holy when you kissed my cheek
Just as you asked to see me again soon
I woke up as afraid of meeting you
As I am of not ever doing so
My faith needs stretching again I suppose
I've written you so well, my little song
Surely you live only in fourteen tens
"Since in a net, I seek to hold the wind"
Preserving you in my saltwater prayers
As long as dreams are, I will meet you there

In a calm as deep as your love for me
Awake with you where the sun sleeps
Genius architect of an archetype
Outbids reality for precious time
You make morning jealous for my doting
As its charming arms can't lure me from yours
Slumber on through sunrise my little song
"I've found the one to whom my heart belongs"
One who goes by a name only dreams know
My faith needs stretching again I suppose
An affair with reality guilts me
For you are as real as my love for me
A love transcending rationality
My little song, my sonnet of a dream

mute

We mourned the emotions buried en masse
beneath mute tongues

Maybe if we had thrown ourselves on the casket
A tragic cabinet of questions hung open wouldn't have unhinged us

Maybe if the flowers had come sooner
the doors we could pass through would be as welcoming as inviting

In writing, we could say the things
In private, the things would say our names
In silence, they would perish in a well mud-deep in wishes

Our mourning isn't black enough
Our wailing isn't wild enough
Our words are not enough,
Enough

The emotions get no justice
Aborted
Muted
Where our dreams try to resuscitate us

And our children claw at the soil
With fingers that will tire inches into burial grounds
Mistook as sacrilegious
When they are anything but

Reaching for the feelings in desperate separates starched and pressed

Kneeling in the surrogate rain of our pain

Soaking our prodigy in our poverties of time and energy
I guess it's good for busily building growing things
But the grass is rooted deeper in our emotions than our emotions are in cortex
In context our amygdala will only smile a knowing smile at those secrets, but we will ever be in
Mourning

Till the feeling noise breaks through to us
We will never see a morning
Until the emotions are rescued from the gentle night they've been in
We will ever be in mourning
For the muted

    I honestly could hardly wait for you to get to this poem. This piece was inspired by a beautifully written historical fiction novel that drummed up a conversation with an even more cherished friend about the generations that break with the silent suffering of our ancestors. Respecting that they had their reasons, but living with the results of those reasons, we opt out. We opt for giving our emotions a voice. We choose to give their feelings a voice as well. Out of love. For them and for us.

One

I don't know how to explain this
But, it's true,
I am a luxury
There are a lot of me but not one other me
Like you could have a thousand in dollar bills in your pocket
But you ain't got a thousand-dollar bill in your pocket

I wish I knew how to say this without perceived arrogance
It's just a truthful circumstance

Whatever and however many fish swim the sea
You ain't ever in your life in all of the multiverse
 met a me
In all of his story you might find similar but never a simile

I am one in a million and a million to one are the odds
That anyone out here is as me as I
And where demand exceeds supply
By definition that makes me
Luxury

A finer thing
Exclusive
Exceptionally

     This one is meant to be humorous play with the hubris oft assigned to a woman who is confident in her singularity. Individualism is an inalienable right of all humans great and small. Enjoy it, BeLoved. Get some on you, but not too, too much.

Legacy

I'd met her but we were never properly introduced
In my youth, she showed up too early for my maturity to match
She never forgot about me
She visited to check up on me
Proceeded carefully till she matched wits with me
Rather I matched wits with a faithful witness
Able to recognize the Faithful Witness
I suppose she figured out it was a good time to not abandon me
My legacy

Plein Air

A plein air prayer
Playing footsie with the earth
Equal parts heart and heaven
"So", I asked her,
"When you went to the place
The place your happy resides
Did you find it where you left it
Was everything left just as you like
Tell me, my darling
What did you find?"
"I found", said she, with eyes twinkling
"That I had brought all the happiness
Every bit of it with me"

    Plein air painting is the act of painting outdoors. More than that, it is abandoning the notion that an environment needs control to be suitable for the artist to capture and interpret the art of it. It allows the artist a freedom of fluidity. Happiness happens this way. When we don't seek to capture and control it but to experience and share it.

Heart

She has heart
Haven't you heard
Her heart is her head
Her head is wholly holy
And her heart led by hands
having held her heaviest
Holds her in higher regard
Hurrying her half steps towards hope
From horror
No halo
She is heart hewn from hollows
Equal parts human, hummingbird, and honeysuckle
Haven to the hapless
Heaven harnessed between her helix and hyoid
Hums hymns for those who haven't heard
She has heart

Earth

Take your time with her
Like God did
She is not to be rushed
She's to be eagerly anticipated
And patiently awaited

She is the curve of infinite angles
Should you see rounds
Ovals and circles
Give her time
She is worth it

Once all the infinitesimal edges
Come into vision
The time is right to proceed with caution

Explore the ambitions toward the horizon of her
Steward her purpose
Champion her forces

Position yourself on the inside of her fortress
Note all the trees in her forest
Copy the delicate balance of water

Gently provoke showers but never churn storms
Respect the gift of being in her midst
To do all of this
you'll need to take your time with her
Like God did

This poem is about the earth. No. Really. Striking resemblance aside. The earth always reclaims herself. We should only take what we can give. And we should always, because we can only, take our time.

Earth reclamation

Earth takes back what's hers
invasive plants of glass and steel
Steal sunshine and ravage parched ground
Drowning alive the fibrous variety
Burning in the wake of its want
Strangling surrounding life
Impractical but
Earth takes back what is hers

The salty brine
The sun over time
Coax the sands to genesis
Erasing lines and starting again
The heavens rinsing the smell of mown down mankind
The clouds carrying fresh, clean, and soft life for the first time in so very long a time
No longer having to be nose deaf to do the job
The burned atmosphere adorns itself with a promise that won't be twisted into protest
Or truth spurned
Earth takes back what is hers

Rust, roach, rat
Each reach back and consume the paths
The roads rambling like ivy
Ivy competitively reclaims
The wisteria in North American southern states
Wisk away brick and mortar
Wish away immortal dreams of metal beams
The earth takes back what is hers

River

You'll find no salt in these waters
They come not from the sea
The weathered storms
Deposit the dissolution of life in me

Ask not why the ocean is blue
But why the river brown
Traversing mud, decay, and silt
To bring life back around

You'll find the path a river carves
Curious and defiant
Patient, triumphed
Through every rocky storm
Mineral and memory rich
Fresh and sweet

Filtered of the residue
Abandoned to her arms
True is the river holding
All entrusted to her bosom

Never wavering in her mission
A constant conveyor of all that's lost
To make sure that it isn't

      This piece is not about a river. When staring at a body of water like a river, I marvel at what that body's purpose is. How well it fills out its purpose and its symbiotic relationships to the environment. The women I'm privileged to know are capable at this in a wa y that is executed with artisan craftsmanship. My deep admiration for our role and our purpose is meant to be expressed in this metaphor.

HERmonally

Thoughts race 'round roads
Diverging
Splintering sprints forward toward checkered pasts
High speed chases
Racing logic to a bridge that ices before
safely crossed roads
Racing solace to abridge out a head of time
Mine is yours and what's yours is undermined
Yielding for flashing lights out
Roundabout patterns part ways with patience
Traffic is always rushed at this our right of way
Highway robbery
Rob me of me and we crash
Hermonally
Rogue

      In all fairness, our hormones don't get a lot of credit where credit is due. When hormones are out of balance, they get our attention in the worst ways, but when they're in balance, we don't applaud the hormones responsible for more energy, less stress or anxiety, elevated mood, sharper mind, and a deep, restful, rejuvenating sleep. Maybe that's part of why they go rogue.

Never satisfied

The doctor's eyes over n95
A strange marriage of condemning and pleading
Unite the estranged
carriage of clinical manifestations
Affirmations of things I know
One thing I don't
But I do, but I don't
As high as the numbers rose
No surprise
This is the life of a woman
Sacrificed to satisfy

I believe in the fate I make
My decision to claim myself as a prize
Means I do what it takes to save my life
Really save my life
No hyperbole in these lines
This is prose as a poem
This is non-fictional telling of the moment
I'm no longer satisfied
Being a lame sacrifice
Basted in cortisol
Turned on a spit
Flame spat upon to roast to a crisp
Balancing harrowing
Between strong black woman and angry black woman-ing
High heat exhausting the palatable me
I've acquired a taste for a life I like
Discarding the lifelong practice of being
Never satisfied

I've been sleeping on you

You know I ain't sleepin' on you
But I've been sleeping
on you
The peace of you on me is restful
Calm

Honorably
You move like the shallow breaths of daydreams
Showers of spring rains in December
You distinctly distinguished thing, you

Vanquish dangerous habits by simply vanishing from where they inhabit
You take me away
Without subtracting me
We make a way
Where none was previously

Stepping in time to a jazz scat
spiritually rhyming with me
Decently
You bested the rest of my life with a look
The rest of my life looks like a book open to my favorite part
since you started parsing my poetry for your rhythm
Dancing two steps of understanding
Twirl and dip them passionate pens like a pianist's chop sticks
Our energy is just just
Every moment a memorable movement

I'm crushed on the mood of you

Frequenting your frequency in solitude
I'm with you
I'm not in love but under the weather of it
As it pours, shines, and blows
Peace is me as rest is you
I haven't been sleepin' on you
But I've been sleeping
On you

    Oooh the sleep when being well loved! Right?! Whether it comes from within or without, it's a rest like none other to feel cared for honestly and openly. Not being ignored or undervalued. What? This piece is about sleep. If you got something else out of it, that's on you. I have nothing to add to that conversation.

I heard a rumor

I heard a rumor I am fearless
Because less full of fear is how you'll find me

Fear for the foreign matter was taking my future by storm
I heard a rumor I am for this
I won't conform

Confirmation is in my delighted defiance
A forgone conclusion that tomorrow itself has actually always been the promise
for those with the fortitude to find it

I heard a rumor I am fearless
And now I can't unhear it

The rumor railed against reason
I adopted and accepted the benign embers
So much fire for a watery being like me
I made steam

The rumor was
It was smoke

Distilled vapor rose in raindrops
In condensating conversation compensating for the thin air up here

Ruminating on the rumor
Till it rooted from a splinter
Entered a dragon slayer
The Spring for every Winter

I heard a rumor I am fearless
Because less full of fear is how you'll find me

Fear is a foreign matter
I'm taking my future by storm
Confirmation is in my delighted defiance

A forgone conclusion that tomorrow itself has actually always been the promise
for those with the fortitude to find it

I heard a rumor I am fearless
And now I can't unhear it

I'm there

I'm there
As there as one may get in this side of here
I'm where the sonnet matures to soliloquy
I am more me than I've ever been
I am more visible than invisible when
My voice sounds just like my Father's love
Enough is my evergreen glow up
I don't take it off
I'm forever young
My womanhood needs no defense for how I choose to define it
My womanhood takes no offense
I'm reminded
The child-like empress
Reigns nonetheless
Absent argument
Present statement of intent
And the Queen don't come off the throne
To debate peasant mindsets

I'm all manners of visceral
I go inside for air
It's comfortable in here
Where poetry is what I eat, sleep, and wear
Where the crossroads of infinite mobius strip me bare
I'm there

Polite, not flirting

It is a truth universally acknowledged, that a single man in possession of a good fortune, must be in want of a wife. Elizabeth Bennet, Pride and Prejudice, Austen 1813

With a kindness hailing from pre-turn-of-the-century chivalry
Soul-stripping brown eyes that burrow internalizing immortal-like
Never anything more powerful than a yielded hand that won't but can
A marbling of might and meekness; a darkly beveled night light
Polite, nice
A stark cry from heirlooms and legacies
Not even a little bit like an invitation to eternity
Not even close to flirting

    It seems to me that it's an awful inconvenience that the rare honorable man whose intentions match his behaviors must suffer the injustice of being misunderstood for it. When it happens to me it sure is.

I can't

I would like to, but I can't
Go for a run alone to clear my head
Clear my throat of the complaints
Anew minute by minute
That look like resurgence
As tired as you are of hearing them
I'm tired of swallowing them

I hide my shape
My voice
My thoughts
I hide from people determined to figure me out without an invitation in
I'm not interested in
entertaining your curiosity with clones
Or your weird fetishes for anybody's business but your own
Ew

I would like to,
but I can't

Travel alone without ammunition or
Hyper vigilance

Jason Bourne doesn't scope out a room for security like me

Bryan Mills' skills ain't particular as mine when I'm trying not to be mistaken for easy prey for some guy

Hawkeye's superhuman ability to spy out the vicinity has nothing on my sensitivity to dangers lurking

I would like to, but I can't insist on respect
Demand honorable treatment in these streets

I would like to go to Cabo and return unmolested by envy
I would like to hope that any country would think me worthy of being returned home to my family
At the very least, pursuing justice for me
To unleash my smile and not be victim of mistaken identity
My smile is not an invitation to pirate my booty
Piracy is a federal crime in the entertainment industry
Where pirating the plagues of young women is most rampant
I can't help but wonder if there's a message in the asymmetry
Amused by the abuse of powerless is symptomatic,
I'm sure of a greater evil than should be named

I would like to, but I can't
Produce children with only the plans of a schoolgirl playing with babydolls
Or to use as a plan for retirement
The burdens on them breaking their stride into their own life

I would like to, but I can't
Relax in my feminine softness
Relinquish any masculinity
Just say thank you and move on
Would you like to see the complimentary scars
Of the compliments before
Would I show you

I would like to, but I can't

I planted peonies in the raised beds
So I wont smell the stench of them

The decayed now feeds flourishing plants

Growing big and fat off every can't

The R-nought of abuse - An Essay and a Poem

Are not the human and the dignity
Part and parcel to one truth
Are not a separation of these
Outright rejection of the proof

Succumbed to the death of innocence
Accepted this as if we have outgrown it
Poor us with our porous reasoning
Entertaining the ideas that what's real is fluid

It isn't

Like a virus that attacks sacred, pious
Merriam-Webster says reverent
Oxford's says hypocritical liars
Even our dictionaries disagree on diction

Evidencing our sickness
Replicating stringent sanctions
Protecting perversions and pain
Quarantining for herd immunity

It will all come to nought
Brought to this place sans peace
History abandons us to infection
Reproducing

Symptomatic suffering
A contact rash of four phalanges
Rosacea and deep tissue soreness

Registering bone deep

Asphyxiating on airborne anger
Memory loss of what we lost
When rage has center stage
Scarring our happiness

Fracturing our hope
Ratios over time risking that all purity will be consumed
Are not the human and the dignity
Part and parcel to one truth

The R Naught of abuse

White vanned

In film, it's always white
The color, ironically, Hollywood horror is washed in
Anonymously ominous
Obvious that its overtly obscure
A vacuum the vulnerable disappear in
A portable crime scene orbits locally
As heavy as gravity on a fallen star
Nearly invisibly to the eye
a chain of evidence dissolves in bureaucracy
As careful as careful can be
Protecting the carriers but not the cargo
The cars go by and no one notices
The vanishing
White vanned into oblivion

Smile responsibly

A smile partially responsible for global warming
Sometimes shy, but mostly
Open
Inviting
Full and full of promise
Thirty-two stars emblazon beastly conditions with angelic semblance
It's just common sense
That it can't be on display 24/7
Yet, there is always some ign'ant body
Tempting fate talkin' 'bout
"Smile, Pretty"
Unaware she's trying to stave off catastrophe
Talkin' 'bout
"You're too pretty to look so mean"
"What's wrong, Baby"
The atmosphere would cave with a steady exposure to her happy
Are you kidding me?
Leave that woman alone
She's just trying to smile responsibly

    Don't you love satire? I love satire! What does it say that a thing as benign and friendly as a smile can be a trigger for alarm in the wrong hands? Imagine being disenfranchised of the choice to display how you actually feel. Wild, right?

Grip

Gripping her womb like that's the place he's missing from
In reality it's someone's womb he's missing
Choking in a part of her chest not responsible for airflow
But, combustible,
 ergo, fire breathing
The absence of him makes her feel even more homeless, cold
Him not being here makes her feel like it's she who wandered away
Wanting a way to hold on
No matter where she goes,
she remains at the place that reminds her of the forbidden tears
that begged him to stay
When her voice lost its way; lost its grip and didn't actually say
He was the only person she'd ever thought to say it to, though
But for him there would be no point to
He slipped into null
Voids constricting constructive junctions
Pausing for words that might take her forward
Father, I forgive you for you know not what you've done
You don't know the measures gone to
Filling feelings with fillers and additives
Attempting to preserve a memory of you
Showing me what it's supposed to look like
to love my life
Showing me that I had a room in your mind
Showing me how to accept emancipation
When love pardoned my misdemeanors
You missed the meaner years
They held me in a chokehold grip
I tried to write this story without you
But I am no story without you

Or my love for you
Daddy, you are not my issue
And I've taken every precaution to ensure your issues aren't either
Neither here nor there but I used to have so much trouble biting my lip
Yet somehow, in letting go of it, I got a grip
Every word that exits, brave and bold or fumbling trips
Massages the pressure
loosening the torque
With a tongue that isn't as tactless as it once was
when it was wound too tight 'round time passed
I got a hold of now
Satisfied with the way I fit in it
Gripped

I'm proud of you

I want to tell you how proud I am
How I know it doesn't mean what I want it to mean
that you hear it from me
But it means something more than vanity
And I wish you could know

I hope that my sincerity is loud enough
and that you remember where it comes from
A place of admiration for your position and your creative independence
A place of respect and love

I might be out of order to say so
And I won't
Though I know that you know
In the quietest quarries
How your existential quandaries are calmed by knowing
that your qualifications are solid

And, that cross pollination makes honey
And Honey, you are
And I'll be
Silent partner to your success
Watching to see which of my prayers for you God may bless
You deserve this
Maybe you didn't, but today you did
And tomorrow you will

Still the negatives and progress in the distance from less
Like I showed you

And give God credit for this
That you gave him some action to bless
I'm proud of you
My pride in you
Resides in you

So, understand, I take only a little for myself
A little less selfless of me to claim this
And I do so silently
Another prayer I breathe in secrecy
Because there is one ear understanding

My happiness in your success is pure and true
and I
am immensely
proud
of
you

Public service announcement to all the friends of the man who had the affections of my heart:
He was special
Now he's not
I'm not pressed to refill his spot

Not because I'm so broken over what was lost
That I could never replace him in my heart

But because I was whole before I met him
So, I went back to whole when we parted
as friends
So please don't get the thought in your head that because I liked him
I'll settle for you instead

He was special and now he's not
But there is no vacancy to fill
No slot
Requiring urgent backfill
There's the life I love and it's full enough
I don't know what it is you thought

    This was a weird one to write. I've only experienced it once and am still in disbelief. I believe in love. Genuine and monogamous. Having survived attempts at it, the notion of trying on humans as if sizing clothes or sampling mall food is upsetting to me. The notion that anyone must be interested in everyone, because of their interest in someone is preposterous. I was young once and thought otherwise. Sure glad that's over!

Arguing

While arguing with thunderheads for enforcing a curfew
I thought of you

You were something of a storm brewing
And I, like, there was nothing better to do,
Thoroughly enjoyed chasing you

They think it rebellious that a lady would tell you this
But cowardice was a curse word when I was created
I unlearned the bad habit of shrinking back
Not long after your storms abated

What cumulus accumulated
Arguments accompaniment to weather phenomena
Brought strong gusts of fury
But that dissipated
I managed

Ruminating over the damage
To put together a decent bit of serenity
I chase clouds back to your vicinity
Swearing them to secrecy

What we go on about's
Between them and me
I only want you to remember me
Arguing
With thunderheads
Because I was never one to make it hard but never one to give up
and give in

The grievous gray looming doom and gloomy
In my Carolina blues won't do it for me
I like my blues more baby, less bullying
My clouds more like streamers of cotton candy
Or bright white looms of cotton creating landings, heavenly
Handing me gently the news of rain
Notwithstanding my tolerance for pain
Not hovering over me harshly like what I have to say
Don't matter
Thundering and striking with agitation
Is weather I weather like a challenge to accept spit hand and shake on
Throwing a tantrum
You're hardly the maelstrom to put fear in me
That's probably why I thought of you
While arguing
With thunderheads for enforcing a curfew
Cutting short my sunshine
Unprovoked
And they can get the last word so long as I get the echo
No, I don't want rain checks and I owe you
No good here
All good year
Traction in my tread makes for non-skid
drifts hydroplaning with a surface tension unbroken in my eyelids
My teardrops tango with raindrops rare
I let them
Better to let a little saltwater out than unchecked air
That's what I tell the changing pressure
When they referee the arguing
With thunderheads for enforcing a curfew
Much like you used to

Toxic relationships have been pop culture beyond a reasonable expiration date. This is not a poem about arguments that are abusive and belittling, though. It's about the sweetness of matching wits with someone who respects and appreciates that you do. It's charming. Endearing.

Easy beauty

The kind that abducts air ducts
Reflexively seeking collar bone support
So sound becomes impossible
He's utterly beautiful
Invited into his vulnerable
His words are second skin to me
If he's a mystery
It's only to them
His extremes trespass with impunity
So familiar in every gradient
Radiant
He radiates as much poetry in his little finger
As all the world's libraries
Silencing rivalries
I'm pretty sure his utterings are soundtrack to a poem's dreams
Every note
Hi to low
Even and especially when a string breaks
Breaks poetry's heart
Before it vanishes into the assonance of deeper sleep
Banishes the dissonance
A restful reap
And still
Poetry fights for just five more minutes to sleep with his sound in its inner ear
I feel like poetry would mind
If he would let himself find time to be possessed
Mine
I don't ask it to share him with me
I sit in awe and rub some in

Settling for absorption
He is utterly beautiful
Uttering beauty easily
His words make the heartache easy
A heartbreak appealing
A romance too pretty for words
For words fall like florals
To the floor where jaw sits salivating for more like
His sound ground down resistance
And
Worlds collide on purpose
To form moons
A dance of luminescent destruction constructing new
He's beautiful
Easy

Weeping body

You haven't the slightest clue how it tears into my skin from within
when you hold it all in
So much pain roils beneath your rage beneath the strength you've
made up your face with
I can feel you when I can't even see you
Only the weeping coursing through you
The weeping you would use to break me against rocks to keep your
secret
I won't tell
Weeping that's bruising the bones of you
You're so tender to touch
You say ouch to love
Squinting under the breaking bright dilating

You haven't the slightest clue how it tears into my skin from within
that I cannot hold you even if my arms do
Give you space for the human alienated from you
You are buried beneath silver
Surfing a beacon you beg for an angel to answer
You pray none comes for the signal
Since the only angels you've ever entertained were the fallen ones
Since they feel more like home in your weeping bones
And you've told yourself God cannot love you
While you try to deny that you say it
In weeping whispers that rage roaring you hear only a welcomed
death approaching
Warring against the survivor you are
Instead of palming prayer
Palming your face with pulsating fury
You punish your body for weeping

You haven't the slightest clue how it tears into my skin from within
that I cannot convince you that I've witnessed the rapids calm quiet from a single command
You just need to tell him you're tired of being a refugee in your body
Where weeping colonies evict your native sun
Where you cannot be reached for all the rage pooling round
You have made a face for it
A face disguising pain as strength
But it runs rampant
A rampage damned to be dammed in dermis

You haven't the slightest clue how it tears into my skin from within
that being strong means freeing the weeping body from the dam you've trapped it in
The bruising contouring the landscape of you has only enhanced your beautiful you're not beyond benevolence, Beautiful
Breaching the weeping body is a violence of release
Relieving the soldier of duty and ending tours tearing up worlds in search of home
Swim where you've surfed surging streams of consciousness
So palpably tangible in the cast shadows of your bones weeping
Worry not that you will be left less than in the vacation of the weeping
For you have always been enough in just your skin
You haven't the slightest clue how it tears into my skin from within
when you hold it all in
But I've a body that weeps, too
It weeps every time for you

And I don't know

And I don't know who these tears are for
Because death is a door-to-door salesman
Devoted to his quota
But for some reason he only pitches on the porches of my friends and family members
I hurt for them

Feeling jealous of the peaceful rest of those sleeping in death
And that's on days when I know for sure I'm not depressed so
I don't know who these tears are for

And I don't know whose tears these are
Am I crying the pent up frustrations of generations watching me pull away from the scar tissue that binds us
Angrily aiming at finishing my breakfast so I can move into the next rung of promise and purpose
Perturbed
Returning frequently to kiss them gentle reaffirming that I don't love them less by loving me more
Are they the tears of my skin so long abandoned
Orphaned of my own affection
Rejoicing to be rinsed of this dereliction
A baptism of sorts
And I don't know whose tears these are

And I don't know if the tears truly stop
Only that they go through longer periods of drought
Trickling along dehydrated ducts
Awaiting weather systems to refill and flush
If I dig deep enough

There's always a trench
Walls soaking wet from the slightest touch
Deluge undamming writers block
Full stop
Carriage return
New paragraph
Paradise shifting paradigm
Composite relief and delight
A day where faith can rest in peace
Rest assured that the things hoped for are copped
And I don't know if the tears truly stop

I can Teach

I can't teach you poetry
It'd be like teaching the heart to call back every beat lost to held breaths
I can't teach you art
It would be like teaching the earth to retrieve oxygen from the gasps of hunters hearths
The way rivers cry drunken history till oceans throw up the skies cries
That is would be what it would be like,
if I tried to teach you poetry
I can't teach you to read the legend to maps of dead spoken language
The symbols of delightful anguish as the art of communication goes the way of Latin
I can't teach you to taste in technicolor
That sweet is a firework that lingers longer in the palate with heat or sour
Can't teach you to hear that one star twinkle louder than any other
I can't teach you poetry
I can't teach you the grace of falling to a stand that won't kneel
I can't teach you to remember your birth in the touch of a lover's hand or find purpose in the caress of a heel
I can't teach you to embrace a minute and squeeze hours from its seconds
I can't teach you that doing so won't bleed them dry but just the opposite you'll bleed them full and rich; lush
I can't teach you poetry
I can't teach you to picture a private audience with God in gardens
To get goosebumps from black swans freshwater ballet
I can't teach you the waltz of winter and spring

Or the music of dying ocean forests coming to life again
I can't teach you to live once you've died, but that's what it would be like
I can't teach you poetry
Or can I?

Pained prettily

Clutching comfort so close
The plumage betrays her pretty
She might prevent the rattling of the train to stop the pain of notice
Beauty is a bully with a particular violence
Pushing forward and with bravado
Demanding to be seen and heard
Declaring itself despite protest
Cradling the naked esteem
As pride yanks at it
The exposure to cold not definitively external
And it's a pretty shame
Everywhere she goes an undertow follows
She's not here to be the lapping tide tickling toes
She is the riptide that tries your every belief in what little control you think you own
Tucks and rolls you deep and down
Careful parallels might feel safe
The thrill of the challenge pulls in waves
She makes the sky accomplice to her game
The sun flirts with diamonds surfaced on her shallow; enticing
The moon's power magnetizing
from abyss to crest dragging basins beneath
Inciting an uprising
She is irresistible urge and ache in ebb and flow
She is a relative rhythm rocking inner child
She laughs when they call earth mother
It's she who nurses every tear year-round
Her leaking from every effort expended a saline expenditure of global proportions
She is birth of worlds worthy galaxy-like expansion
She is infinitely more than what she is not

Pretty

If you tell me I look pretty
Be prepared for me to show you my ugly side
It's nothing personal
Just how I learned to survive
Pretty pokes holes in peace
Hunts my haunted pieces
Scarier than mortality
Pretty pangs me
I prefer epiphanies in place of Tiffany's
Cartier cards the day and finds it forever young
But would you still love me when I'm no longer
Young and beautiful
You know what's pretty
My ability to stand here and ask you not to abuse my trustful nature politely

When sugar boils

That rich dark caramel don't come easy Sis
The dissolution of your sweetness
A concentrate superheated
Requiring full attention

If you leave it
You can forget dessert and the pan you cook with
Smooth swirling of sugar hydrated
Patient

It should boil but not boil over
Keep the temps at just enough pressure
Not to break with peace but to release the sweet
Amber waves of rich decadence
When sugar boils

    Stay sweet. Stay palatable. Mostly for you. Somewhat for them. My younger self would find this laughable and maybe start a sentence like, "But they [hurt] me first!" How does one apply pressure to pressure? Push back. Not with what pushes you, but with what you're made of. That's more than enough pressure.

Things she wants you to know

She is created with a need for your lead
You needn't tell her she's needy
As if it's greedy to have basic needs met
And, on this point, it's counterintuitive for you to give her regrets

She was born at war just like you
She fights wickedness with a smile
You can forgive her a few lipstick smudges and other war wounds

Her combat ready fatigues are as appropriate as yours for the occasion
She wants to be free not to camouflage in your presence but
Whatever she's wearing, she's dressed in excellence
Because she needs you the way a model needs a tailor
Not to make her but play up her features
Expert in the craft to measure words twice so no damage is done in the cut

Favoring and enhancing her fabric with an informed eye to her
Features unseen to the naked eye
But never more naked than when seen eyes wide shut

Because she needs you not the way a daughter needs a father
Not the way an engine needs a starter
More like the way the earth needs water
So if you got nothing but dry emptied wells
Well, don't bother

She gets it from her mother
Whether you like it or not

She also takes after her father
Be careful how you shoot your shot

That walk you admire has two meanings
First, she can but, if she shouldn't, yet she must,
she will and she has
But when she does, she will let go of your hand
and not look back
Second, yes it's exactly like that

She's not inflicted with false modesty
And offers no apology for her gifts and blessings offending your insecurities
But she 'o'nt mind offering tutoring if need be
Cause she practice what she preach

You can put that on everything
If you're a gambling man
They say never bet on red
She is well read, misread, and much too valuable a message to be left on read

You should always reply like you mean love
You should oftentimes be first to call
You can be her answer even when you don't know it all

There's just a few things she wants you to know

She is looking for a reason to
When all the reasons she knew
are off the table
Hope floats but so does truth
Where they float together is where she hopes to find you

Where they separate, she will too

He didn't ask

Testosterone spiked entitlement
Straight no chaser
Blurs reasoning
Slurs judgment
Drunk off patriarchal punch
A hard case of misogynistic munchies
Overwhelming impulses touches
Places that won't come clean in a bath
He didn't ask

    A question is a powerful tool. Don't think you automatically can or can't have what you like or do what you like because the parties contingent upon you having or doing it must approve the request. It's a blessing and a privilege to be granted access to what we like. Not an entitlement. There's nothing wrong with that.

Future

Future, will you wait for me
Please
I'm sorry but not sorry
I had things to do
Things I needed from me
For me to be ready for you
Now I finished my breakfast and lunch, too
I put dinner on and it'll be a few hours
I couldn't meet you where I was
You weren't there
I couldn't beat you where you are
Science hasn't made it that far
But, could you wait for me
I'm coming
I was caught in traffic behind obligations
The past outstayed it's welcome one, four, 10 times
I was stuck holding baggage for some ancestors of mine
But I'm on my way
Not the on the way that means I'm thinking about what shoes to put on, then I'm heading out
But I'm fully dressed and I left the house
On my way home to you
Just need you to
Wait for me please

Triggered

Passed away in a sizzling heat almost imperceptible
Just hot enough to uncomfortable
It singes the spidey senses numb
Swallowed by the rage geyser spouting nonsense over everything
salty and too hot for comfort
Lumbering 'round overwhelmed by sound and sight
Fleeing the fight from me
Searching for respite

Hard

Hard knowing I could've been your completion if you didn't see me
as competition
Hard watching your pupils disappear behind disappointment
The things you find most important
hold no weight with me whatsoever

I wanted to make it matter
I wanted to make it all better

My life expectancy exculpatory evidence of possibility
My experience doesn't define yours, though
Nor should it
I get it but I don't
Because I don't get it
But you do so that's fine
for you
But it's hard

When I have full enough heart in the sum of its parts
To seed with its shards a yard full of perennial summer flowers
But winter is your favorite season
I asked for a reason, but your axis couldn't be reasoned with

In spite of spatial reasoning
You spun out of orbit of anything I'm good at
It's hard but knowing you'll never again look at me like that
Like the instant before the decloaking of the science of art

Remember when you needed to know
You shredded the lid of Pandora's box to get at its insides

Now, at the sound of my hopeful voice you hide
That's odd

Hard that my apology isn't the one you'll accept because it isn't the one you deserve
And justice won't be served when I offer but forgiving yourself is a harder lesson learned
And you were not ready when our chances were
You got the woman everybody wanted then remembered you ain't everybody

When you looked at me and saw your insatiable mother
Your demanding father
You didn't bother questioning the dove's cry
Wiping the dove's eye to peer inside the windows of a winged thing for healing
You put your implicit trust in the flight of broken love

And it's hard to know you couldn't trust a real one
Just because it's foreign, so I say I'm sorry to and for the unforgiven
Hard dissolving what would've been resolution given more insight, more patience

Making it make sense and make dollars
Shoot, could've built an empire
The fire for building bricks is the same that burns it down
I asked you to match purpose instead of outfits
You turned me down

It's hard
Watching you match wits with something that appears beneath you
A conduit to my intuition a strange feeling like I'm watching you settle into Van Gogh's blue period
Wondering which ear will go next as you cut off your nose to spite

your face

Wishing I could infuse courage to your veins

Maybe I'm just being vain
To want to make you as comfortable in the humidity of me as in the artic tundra of malaise
We are worlds apart and it's
Hard

I'm not her

She is a marvel of mystery
a model of beauty and brains
She is the uncharted
polarized to everything except the blood in your veins
She is your antihero
Saving and slaughtering you
Condemning and exonerating you
Thrilling toxicity traps you in flames
You need to burn to feel safe now

Quenching sounds like lynching with a noose of boredom
Peace sounds like drawing and quartering
You don't trust happiness any further than the leash she let you loose on
Patience is a narcoleptic nightmare
Truth stings like sunburn on your sensitivities scraped raw from tongue lashings
And excitement is an ice cream cone on the pavement
A slap and a kiss are synonymous
A laugh feels like spilled bubbles in tall grass

The option of loving you obliterated
The available access is shuttered
Cupped closed behind her closed palm
closed pinched disappointed lips

All you've ever needed is her
Alas, I am not your mother

Shame

Shame is a beautiful and daring thing
It accessorizes and complements
Our modesty
Not meant to be stitched into every seam
But lacing the corset of contentment to minimize complacency in egregious things
To be undone by forgiveness and confidence in a moral compass
But shame has been given a bad name
Abuse of it has weaponized a useful and gainful process
Please be careful where you aim it

    I don't subscribe to the belief that any of our feelings are vestigial garbage we don't need. Shame, like any tool can be weaponized, but I am proud when I feel ashamed of behaviors that hurt. I don't feel the need to define what that looks like for others, but only to advise that maybe we're being a little too hard on ourselves to throw away any part of ourselves that we feel by design. Instead of acknowledging its message and behaving accordingly.

Indestructibly you

I posit that losing oneself in a performative identity is partially the reason for so many tragedies
There's too many people "acting like themselves"
Never making acquaintance with their actual self
Performing under duress i.e. or else
Or else the so-called friends their caricature made throw shade at the integrity of the character wading
quicksand in slow motion through a shadowed life
In a darkness too opaque to light the trail of falling star dust
Taking umbrage at the upstart's upstarrus composite
Self-righteous judges indicting the innocent of charges they can't acquit themselves of
And it's stressful
To be who the panel of "They" want you to be
And who "They" don't
When their mood fluctuates and flood gates open over the man-made mountains of molehills

I posit
You can be you still...

There's a place for you where all you have to do is manage your own expectations of who
What
How
You are
From afar
No need to lose awareness that among us walk opinions and persons whose feelings matter
You'll have a better grasp on which is the former or the latter

You'll be your own ally in a battle for identifying
And anyone beside you will be an asterisk
Very little risk
Reduced need for defensiveness
Reduced stress over common flex
Standing a ronin amidst a garrison of comparisons
No one can make you a motif against your wishes
No one can downgrade your belief to what your character isn't
Your power is as full as your faith is
You have the onus
On us the accountability to own us
And with that our happiness
However you were raised
Too little or too much praise
Days gone by are not relevant to the equation
From here on out you're ambassador of your embassy
You being the sum of your deposits

    I give a talk called Indestructibly You. It focuses on retaining the identity we make for ourselves when outside forces are against it. Most of the women I have the pleasure to know are working on being her best self in the face of generational trauma, valid fears, deficits of role models, etc. But she is aiming for more. More gracious. More courageous. More confident. More peaceful. More flexible when she should be and less so when she shouldn't be. More aware of when she isn't.
    What we don't talk about enough is that becoming is an infancy stage. Giving ourself grace to stumble into maturation and giving those around us grace as they deal with our infant stage requires us to be, as Jesus Christ is quoted at Matthew 18:4, like a child. You ever notice how children roll with the punches? They are quicker to accept what is without adopting it as a personal attack.

And Let's Not Forget

She was born not Princess, not heir apparent, but Queen
believing both sky and earth are home
Gravitating and levitating
Nothing living can match the levity of that woman's hope
She grew up duct taping molted feathers into makeshift wings
Like air current she can make just about anything shift
Without an assist
She just didn't know this

That was then

When she noticed it, she bodied it

Know this

She's a slow kiss rushing like blood to the head
She's a wish echoing in the heart chambers where your life gets its best acoustics
She's where every endorphin goes to rest and re-emerges as zest
She blankets the transactional with ephemeral ecstasy
She is everlasting but ever so brief
So, while she is present make the most of it

She's as close to perfect as the now can get
Rummaging through your raggedy for a reason
Making one, if need be, out of salvaged bits
Know this
And let's not forget
Pained Prettily
Clutching comfort so close
The plumage betrays her pretty
She might prevent the rattling of the train to stop the pain of notice
Beauty is a bully with a particular violence
Pushing forward and with bravado
Demanding to be seen and heard
Declaring itself despite protest
Cradling the naked esteem
As pride yanks at it
The exposure to cold not definitively external
And it's a pretty shame
Everywhere she goes an undertow follows
She's not here to be the lapping tide tickling toes
She is the riptide that tries your every belief in what little control you think you own
Tucks and rolls you deep and down

Careful parallels might feel safe
The thrill of the challenge pulls in waves
She makes the sky accomplice to her game
The sun flirts with diamonds surfaced on her shallow; enticing
The moon's power magnetizing
from abyss to crest dragging basins the beneath does suppress
She is irresistible urge and ache in ebb and flow
She is a relative rhythm rocking inner child
She laughs when they call earth mother
It's she who nurses every tear year-round
Her leaking from every effort expended a saline expenditure of global proportions
She is birth of worlds worthy galaxy like expansion
She is infinitely more than what she is not

They'll Write

They'll write poetry about the colloidal cradle called your eyes
Gasping at and gulping the sinking shape of your history with gravity
The windswept warmth of your tomorrow in their hands
They'll write words to try to carve that feeling into sound waves that tattoo your skin
In hopes you will echo back to them in some way
They'll write poetry to find you in the conclaves of classic art
Your renaissance
They'll recite you
To keep you
To fight you
They'll pen odes to your inescapable energy
enigmatic mood
Clarified purpose
The vastness of your voice
The passionate noise of your promise
They'll write poems to memorialize the wars with you
The ones they win and the ones they'll lose
When they choose you, they'll write sonnets
When they lose you, ballads
They'll write along your contour
They'll write between your lines
They'll rhyme with the time of what you've got beating inside
Woman, woman, WOMAN
They'll write poetry for you and to you
Decrying their vanity over you
Belying their vain illusion of sanity when it comes to you
Crazy
You'll make them crazy
They'll call you crazy

And they'll write poetry about that, too
They'll write mad soliloquies about the maddening tug-of-war for your soul and spirit
Frustrating monologues about distance and desire
Tiring of trying to deny that it's you
Possessing their subconscious with serendipitous fortuity
They'll write poetry about the empty they feel without you
And the drowning they feel beside you
And how they thought they should come up for air
To find, all along you were the air too
Escaping the quill in the volatility of new life
Splashing onto the pages
They'll write

Thank you for traversing the many facets of femininity – the passion, the pain, the grace, and the strength. This book is a tribute to the women who have shaped our lives, inspired us to be better, and shown us that anything is possible when we believe in ourselves.

www.ingramcontent.com/pod-product-compliance
Lightning Source LLC
Chambersburg PA
CBHW071440160426
43195CB00013B/1981